SLOWLY, SLOWLY, HORSES

Julianne Buchsbaum

AUSABLE PRESS
2001

Cover art: *Untitled,* by Kim Schwartzhoff (detail)
Oil pastels, ink, pencil, & marker on photographic paper

Design and composition by Ausable Press.
The type is Bruce Rogers' Centaur.
Cover design by Rebecca Soderholm.

Published by
Ausable Press
46 East Hill Road, Keene NY 12942

www.ausablepress.com

The acknowledgements appear on pages 85–86 and
constitute a continuation of the copyrights page.

Library of Congress Control Number: 2001089398
ISBN: 0-9672668-6-6 (case; acid-free paper)
ISBN: 0-9672668-7-4 (pbk; acid-free paper)

SLOWLY, SLOWLY, HORSES

For my mother

TABLE OF CONTENTS

I.

◇FLUTES IN TUNISIA

The purple mosque casts
a shadow of green
quite far from where we are
or want to be.

Telephone wires
encircle a pole
like electrocuted snakes.
Still we are drawing the pall

over a love
short-circuited long ago.
We should admit that now
we'll never know

why flutes in Tunisia
do not sound the same
as they sound here,
though arsonous flames

consume as quickly
leaves that look like they
were dipped in blood.
As if there were a way

to attune a man's
sleeping tympanum
to thunder and the pules
of wind while from

a fragrant monticule
where once his sultan frowned,
he observes the cloistered
circle of a sleeping town

and lights that fibrillate dimly
in the skin of night.
Even his minions were
unnerved by fright

as waves collapsed at the prow
like torn fans
and corsairs hooted
on the Mediterranean.

◇REASONS

The thought of the moon gives off
the scent of apple-cores.

The actual moon stares like a blind eye.
It takes a long time to see what is there.

Leaves heave in the wind like gills
of dying fish, and water striders

skim the lake's broken chrysoprase.
Nesting in the far hills, the sun

drops glass oranges on the water.
A gray tide surges in your eyes,

its waves chopped by wind, almost
the same wind that disturbs the leaves

and the shadows of leaves by the pier.
I can almost see barnacles cleave

to the prow of a boat foundering there,
anchors clanging, tossed in those waves.

I can almost see your reasons
scattered like shells in the undertow.

Who could find refuge in such fragments?
Through mud the color of ripe plums,

you walk with your hands open
as if to collect the wind's squandered coins.

Out of the south woods a swallow flies,
losing its shadow over the lakewater.

The thought of the swallow vanishes
with the scent of apple-cores.

◈ ACOLYTES

Outside the machine shop,
tufts of bluegrass poke

through chicken wire, scrap
metal, slabs of corrugated

tin. A tractor, frame
embossed with rust, turbo

engine defunct, no longer
chugs from its rut of stasis.

Where it hulks in a patch
of canary grass, chicory opens

pale blue eyes around it.
Torsion of weeds in slight

winds as though absolute
submission were the purest

kind of pleasure. The sun
with its volumes of light in which

we crouch leaf by leaf,
scraping larvae into tin cans,

uprooting weeds, rocks.
And the furrows like tunnels

through which we pass each day
with no way out, as if

to reach the end were atonement,
as if, acolytes of air and light,

we too might fail for want
of soil in which to root ourselves.

❖ MEADOW OF LOCUSTS

Deep in the meadow of locusts, one hears
them churr, thick as rain.
What do they mean by dimpling the air with rasps?

In the nectaries of peaches one tastes sunlight,
dripping all its gold.
The days lumber by, slow as oxen hauling

the heft of a dead tree. In the green air,
the chorus of locusts turns
yellow while milkweed pods split apart and let

fly their cottony fleece in the wind. The sky
holds a corsage of thistle-
clouds, and the air is spiked with sweetness.

The bare branches of a tree veer at odd
angles at the field's edge
like a man flailing his limbs in cold water.

The locusts churr from a different tree, churr
at spotted leaves, the sky,
the wave of shadow that crests on the hill and spills

into the meadow where milkweed tufts
revolve in slow currents.
Sunlight seems to dribble letters on that hill,

to ink on the cragged horizon in hasty cursive
a script too brief,
too fluid to decipher, though the stony profile

of the hill bears up under it without questioning
what it says or what
the locusts mean by disturbing the air with such stridor.

◇ WINNOWING

A spotted fawn stood crookedly
in the corral
while sumac flared on the hills.

Even then it was strange to be alive.
I remember a swimming pool
in whose icy chemical blue

elliptic syllables drowned,
water fountains
in which our reflections fell apart.

Crawdads raking their blotched
claws in the creek
as if to uncover something lost;

the row of hedges under whose
sun-stained leaves
dank shadows seemed to wait for us.

Those days when saddles chafed our legs,
and we learned to ride in lines,
to guide the horses' bridled heads,

and to hear little more voluble
than winds that etched
illegible lines in the fields.

Perhaps the thunder of the visible
gave us pause,
but soon we'd cease to trust ourselves

to hard weeds stubbling the hills.
And need does not name its object;
it only umbrellas and swoons

through trees that house a darkness.
How little it mattered then
how far apart we were

when the dark-scalloped fringe
of leaves along strangulated paths
was enough to transport us,

the guttering campfire a smudge
of Sunday, and the fawn's ears,
a velvet ash, blown back

by wind that seemed a warning,
a winnowing—a sharp breath
belying the scintillations of summer.

❖ CONCORDIA DISCORS

Like the day the river was dragged for the drowned boy
and crows clustered in oaks that seemed to be burning

down along the shore—with the motherhive hatching
and everything the color of catbrier and snakes that curl

in the undergrowth—there is no fire here, no naked
eye, no naiad. The river is waning and in want of rain.

Imagine a man in a car fingering the phosphorescence
of a radio dial, imagine through the rearview mirror

he's watching spring etch the hills in nitrate of lime,
hatch from a reservoir of ice great lumps of scum

and aspergilli. The clouds are high and have no smell.
Let's say the car is left in an overgrown field behind

a mobile home where kids are ruined about the mouth.
Let's say he lays in the cradle of its cold embrace

and becomes to himself a wasteland.
Strange life of profusion, ochre, mourning doves.

As for the drowned, he begins to love nervously or never.
He waits for the sound of burning trees.

His not the hand behind your back, nor is he the fanatic.
He came to see animals ruined about the mouth,

the botched heirloom of biology. The river lost its way
in the lupine, but who bore the brunt of the storm?

◈ PALINODE

It was time to come in from the wind
or didn't you know
below the darkwindowed houses
whose knockers brought
no one to the door as you listened
to the swishing of leaves:
maple, crabapple, oak
deep-rooted in earth
with its texture of rotting nets.
You wished it weren't true,
but the swishing sounded
like a palinode, the leaves ripping
apart their promises
of an hour before, warning you
of more wind and darker
storms roiling over farmlands.
I see the portico where you stood
seeking protection
as though the self could escape
its own bad weather.
I remember the sound of your voice
describing how much more
there could be as trucks plowed
north toward Marengo,
as time clicked its teeth
and scraped each minute
like fingernails down your back.

◇ALEXANDER THE GREAT

Dwarfed by the space between mesas he stands
in dusty boots near junipers crushed by desert light.
The bones of a bob-cat whiten nearby, flensed
by desolations and winds from nowhere and no words.
Then comes the mooncalf flexing its jaws, unhinging him.

They try to dislodge the mooncalf from his mind—
its plaintive lowing keeps him up half the night;
it sucks the milk of his visions; it wastes him.

Cacti spring up along the trail like fat fists
armored with spikes, and he bends with a jackknife
to gut their green flesh for juice, scant and hidden.
With a map and compass he points the way
and they follow, knowing all heroes turn to bone.

Something cruel has tutored him, they think.
The mooncalf keens in his mind and not even
stars can wake him as they stick their hatchets
in the sky and he vacillates between the real world

and the world brotherhood. The clang of sidereal battles
rings in his ears; he is sure his mooncalf is conquering
the cosmos for him, its hooves galloping over novas.

❖ OBSERVATION

Far above the quiet houses
hangs a sac of translucent
gel (a cocoon/a feast/
a nest/an infection?).

All around it black worms
assault its moist skin
(you might imagine
gelatin, a rotten cherry,

a fungal deliquescence).
The worms are quiet,
like the houses,
but not very polite.

Their hard, blind heads
hang from branches
of suburban trees, which
no one climbs or topples.

Next to them a swarm
of beetles has just hatched.
Their faces are huge mouths—
disturbed, disturbing—

come out of their shells
at last with ravening
appetites. They'll devour
every leaf in sight.

◈ JACK OF NO TRADES

I.

These branches are fragments
of a byzantine argument that stems

from an obstinate problem; they end
in a gnarl of leaves, a veined

fusion of hieroglyphs. Overnight, ideas
came to me, but they broke down in the light.

My dreams slipped out the door like frightened dogs.
And down by the river, the ducks

tuck their bills in their feathers,
grass teems with grasshoppers' green spasms

and a snail drags its phlegmatic foot,
quiet as the sun who flings his coronet on the ground.

II.

Leaves hang like dessicated tongues.
I can't revive them.

The sun makes them mustard-colored,
as the world shrivels to a skeleton of what it was.

The sun is too hot for logic,
always striving, everywhere at once.

The leaves start falling as though tired of arguing.
They tell me nothing.

Ivory clouds tusk the sky, and the sky bleeds blue.
Memories flood my mind after months of stagnation;

their freshets irrigate my dreams—
carrying all I'd thought dead and corrupted.

III.

Last night's cologne still lingers on my scarf:
I feel the world squeezed out of me—

with star-infected eyes I see it vanishing.
A chain of rusty freight cars kindles a dream of escape,

but they're stuck on the tracks for now.
The houses look on with reproving stares

and the stars sink back in the sky.
Winter comes on for the jack of no trades

who sits in a thunder of wind.
Grasses poke up like fighters proud of a dingy heritage.

Clouds let go their scribbles of snow;
the sun is too weak to erase them.

❖ BIRDLIGHT

All summer toads croak from ditches,
a scarecrow slumps in a russet field,
and through chinks in the cellar door

darkness leaks like mildew

or the bog-hole blue of cypresses trailing
fronds over the limestone fountain in the park.
The moldy fountain spurts threads of water

like an old woman tired of combing her hair.

And there, under lull of pondscum,
pennies glister—cold, dead goldfish.
From a matrix of blurred branches

emerge the shadows of strangers.

Bits of me flap away in the birdlight.
Behind abandoned houses where the yards
are rife with leafrot and rubbish,

in alleys where dumpsters cradle their stenches,

fear slithers its tendrils into me.
And with that I discover a wilderness
not yet chilled by factory whistles

nor tethered to pendulums of clocks—

just the coiling of eels in a swirl of saltwater.
And what Atlantis had I thought to find here
among the mossy cypresses

with their listless yawing in yellow air?

There is nothing here but a sky
the color of lice in which
a child's blue balloon wavers upward.

❖ LANDSCAPE IN DECEMBER

A greenish skin of ice glitters on the lake
on which a flock of grackles congregates.
Who'd want to sit beneath this statue

caparisoned with canteen and rifle,
this statue who watches
from his stanchioned pedestal in the park

as if it's all the same to him?
Over his dark brow the clouds flow and flow.
Something clangs in dolorous tones.

Winter adjusts its nuances of white;
the city is drenched in fog
that surged in from the lake like a fever.

Quayside stevedores
heave crates from rusty barges
as cathedral bells denote the languid hours.

Clerks walk by on lunchbreak—
their reflections in storefront windows
leap out at them like mistakes they keep repeating.

❖DAMAGED INTANGIBLE

All befores and afters taint this landscape
where a colt stumbles from its mare.

Flies black as seeds in the spoiled fruit I eat.
How will he come to me now from ranks

of brambles, musk of carrion in yards
of honeysuckle, rheumy soil and shades

raven with decay? And then this crisis
of pines in brindled vistas. The passion

of bur oaks and alders, clouds pink-
veined as these already-etiolated purslanes.

If only you could hear it, ear filled with wind.
Clover in fallow fields, uncut, wet with rain.

I'm lost in these rocks, bitter carbonic archives,
trees black with streaks of crows. The difficult

soil already at such angles deprived of the sun.
The colt stumbles toward what will feed him.

Barberries beneath coldfronts shifting northwest.
He'll only come as damaged dreamed intangible.

I could hear him, if only with a wind-filled ear.
Where is the line between here and someday?

The earth turns in its green inertia as I
eat fruit spotted with seeds like black flies.

The colt stumbles into a pasture of taints. Where
is the line between looking and looking away?

◇ CLOUDS SWELL OUT

The finale of fall hangs in yellow clusters.
You can't muster

the drive required for potent acts—to hide
like the cat who eyed

each skittering leaf and churring sparrow from
a dark sanctum,

frozen, invisible, dumb—such is your will.
The world is ill

with demands it can't meet; hence, the crickets'
deaths, the rosettes

of rot, the dusky clusters, and flourishing worms.
All this confirms

your wish to divorce yourself from the vista
and phenomena

of autumn which looms from raw branches a dark
afternoon. The stark

landscape deepening its shadowed dales cannot
stray a lot

from the invincible doctrine, though owls moan
misgivings. Alone,

you watch a jet's contrail zip open the sky
and the high

clouds swell out like huge, snowy hearts disgorged.

II.

❖ INVOCATION

if I could return to the fairgrounds
fragments

would be there   not you
how is it

still for me your whistle divides the evening air
as mourning doves in redbuds start up

their soft complaints their soft complaints their soft
       complaints their

fragments
would be there   not you

how is it

a limestone arch led from a gorge
of shadows to where   you disappeared

if I could return to the fairgrounds
fragments

would be there   not you

◊QUEEN OF ULTIMA THULE

Here in the ultima Thule of my mind,
I no longer think of you. I left you in my sleep,
in the throne I established for you there.
When dawn eased its pallor between the blinds,

my mouth was dry. Far below this mountain
with its ice-cream cool, its undulant planes
and royal blues, I see the shadows teeming.
Dust turns to mud in the yellow rain below.

Once I held a poppy, red as a beggar's eye.
That flower was the oriflamme of my striving.
I crouched beneath the pelting rain while
some new suffering whirled beneath my skin.

And this is the kingdom bestowed on me
by your mouth and its crimes and perils.
Here there are no shadows. At the apex
I tear at with my pick-ax, all is ice and steel.

◇DEAR VAGRANT

Your train departs in ten minutes.
In my version of this traffic
in ache and leakage, you lean into

the valley of the shadow of vandalism.
And the vespers you gesture toward—
their sweetness is almost fetal.

Bring me rubies, Robber Baron,
or a visitation of magpies—
that's when I'd want to marry you,

when cows are gouging up fields
of hardscrabble rye and umbels
blush by the junction box.

Meanwhile, cast those glances
like grenades that burst inside me.
Of the vacuoles that don't add up,

which ones count? Dear vagrant,
if the volatile disturbs you,
remember how soon we kiss

darkness. By noon I'll be odd and
valedictory down where the air
smells of railcars and windstorm.

◇NEW MOON HANGING

Your mouth is not a flower.
Deceptively soft, it does not
allow one word to fall
the way a petal would break

from a perianth.
Nor will it release
your swallowed dreams,
those delinquent visions.

Outside, vagrant geese fly
not into a white and classical
winter sky but into virescent
rainclouds of early April.

Those clouds swell
with bruised colors
as you stitch your life
into little quilted patches.

A dream smashes against
the hull of this moment.
The dream is a shark's fin
from the green gut of the sea

swerving in your direction:
the dark's last stab
at making you listen.
Rain pours down in sheets

that look like screens
to keep things in or out.
Locked inside the house,
you see the storm but not

the tattooed crescent
of a new moon hanging,
absolutely moon-like,
in the blackened sky.

❖ VINYL RECORDS

Halcyon, no—though you could not know then
the deck of cards summer held to its chest

until you stood displaced in orange light,
your mouth awry with words you'd never say.

Cottonwood trees slowly scumbled by gray
shadows, hornets retreating to the eaves,

and papers tumbling in a shift of wind.
Nights when the barn owls blinked

at a jonquil moon, the tasseled corn, slugs
puckering in dust—the country tainted then

by autumn's gruel of sleet. But you would leave
too soon to see the fields shake off their gold;

shut in your room at night, you played a stack
of vinyl records spinning like cracked roulettes.

◇ANECDOTE OF A MANICHAEAN

No character who's kind
in this tale of what the mind
can do to the body.

Life, the old impostor,
sank under the cragged plaster
of its ponderous effigy.

Is it true that ennui
can really be just a need
for water? Mentally

there's a slow inversion:
the self's alarming version
of its enemy.

It went from simple white
to cataclysmic night:
that strange, erratic sky.

The mind can't apprehend
that what should never end
is always passing by.

The body knows the truth
despite its terrified, mute
rehearsal of the lie.

❖GAMBLERS

You doze in a castle of eggshells, Tartar,
while rain soaks the cornfields outside.
This is not about me; I have nothing to do with it.

Who are you, ruminating in the corner like that?
The bar is dark; it's time to go home.
Stop ransacking the past for what ruined you.

See, outside, how the sweet cicely holds
its tiny white umbrellas in the storm?
You thought you were safe here?

Alumroot blanches the roadside from here
to wherever you're going.
Nodules that no one but you knows are alive,

lives that are their own reason for being,
with the whiteness of what is thrown open
to the dead silence of the universe.

While someone faces the hazards of loving you,
the clouds overhead foam like boiling milk
and you turn solemn and cold and formal.

Somewhere the sea drags itself over the faces
of the drowned. Somewhere gamblers
are cutting their losses as another day slips by.

❖ DAYS OF NO LUSTER

The door was well and firmly closed
or so I thought. Pigeons took flight

between stone walls gone soft in fog,
vendors presiding at kiosks.

We touched hands and bought nothing.
I sought to plunder language

as if a word could be a lens
through which to scrutinize the soul.

You pulled me in to taste henbanes
(Thorn Apple, mandragora)

that he who was within could not escape.
How soon you vanished. I thought

the door was firmly closed,
but phobias mushroomed at the root of me.

You took my hand as trees cracked
in the summer storm: imprudent,

I know, but with that, I became a vassal.
The thought of your hands latches and

unlatches me as ambulances scream by
and I lie in the brief gold of seven o'clock.

To walk arm and arm in velvet dark, counter-
pointing days of no luster. Smashed

bottles in the alley below and the word
through which I saw myself has brought me here:

the clock's catarrh raking the air
like a sick old insomniac. August here—

but not in the mind and not for long—
in you my heart's blood abluted.

◇FLAME LOUNGE

This city is waxwork—
when we work, it burns.
And you stand there
in mail-order clothes
from a warehouse in Chicago
where no one knew
the multitude of nights

you would be no one's
shepherd's staff.
The world inherits winter
like a herd of sheep
in a chokehold of fog,
ill-husbanded under
a malachite moon.

I know by heart ten
fragments from the ice age
of our discourse. You
have seen me faithless
and hesitant to enter
my body's chrysalis
of vessels and cells.

I am contagious, I buy
on credit, I don a coat
of Congo red. Once
I saw bronze domes
heliograph messages
of fire and fear across
the city at sundown

and heard a commotion
of boats in the harbor.
I wish I could believe
in alternate universes
where tonight the street-
lamp's sallow nimbus
will be no one's halo.

◆IOWA RIVER, 8/9/99

Summer and the horizontal Babel of a river
flecked with foam, tongues talking at cross-

purposes down the small hours of dew and gray.
Bubbles float over ruined and roan-colored logs,

oblivious to deaths by drowning, blighted, blotting
out the light. Unfurling slow as rust that lurks

for years in cogs and sprockets and finally flowers
forth as if in judgement of junk yards—the tares

of town and country. Summer and the white
ascent of airplanes roaring overhead, desuetude

of railroad tracks. What once was winter
is winter no more, is torrified. Striations of rot,

rootlessness, tongues held still as hunted prey.
Departures in the dead of night, the mockingbird's

mica eye that glints three times and is gone,
the locust shedding its skin outside the depot,

the calyx of blue lobelia breaking in the sun.
What once was enough is enough no more,

learning the light touch of *easy come, easy go.*
Behind a barricade of snakeweed and slowly

as a cornucopia is hoarded, the river brings on
tidings of toxins, foaming through noon and beyond

in its nuance of froth and algae, past boarded-up
windows on the outskirts, the hives of hornets

hanging on and on, the not-dying-off and profligate,
crickets that trill three notes and are over.

◇A HOUSE OF CARDS

I suppose we were dis-
illusioned and chilled,
but what a lovely time

was had by all: a clear
night, early winter,
a party ensuing in the

building next door,
the young valets dashing
down the alley yelling;

an expectation of new things,
the banishment of death
and unmentionables.

We called for an encore
of noble reasoning
in the dining hall, with our

destiny unknown for the night,
and the high loves of
the hostess revealed

to all and sundry—who
danced with the fervor,
that night, of orphans.

◈AWAITING THE WRECK

He hears the forlorn wails of summer loons;
back home, years pass, bureaucrats hatch red tape,

hire lawyers in vain. Their world balloons
with dilemmas, heinous suits; the crass landscape

mutates. Strangers on the street raise their heads
at the boy like water moccasins rearing up

with alien eyes from muddy riverbeds.
Jungle gyms become gordian knots. The stoop

of his mother's brownstone is the fo'c'sle deck
of a ship from which spume of the raging world

cannot wet him. There he awaits the wreck
of night with its crooked pirate flag unfurled.

After a point, he ceases to inquire where
the captains are and pretends not to care.

❖FOLIE À DEUX

A dog lies at his feet as he looks into
his manual and says,
A person reduced to his worst elements

makes a fascinating subject. He refers
to his model with her back
against the wall. In the flat that he has

exiled them to, he is his monster,
he his eaten. Her eyes
are those of a hawk, sharp and unselfconscious.

It is an eclipse of the world:
his ribs
stick out like the bars of a grill.

Everything in the room seems to flow
into everything else:
the dog curling its tail on the orange rug,

the wooden bureau, his black boots,
the smears of green paint
all over the place. He considers the canvas

and rearranges it completely. She sits
like a mound of clay
in shades of grisaille. For there is no way

to confute this swimming iridescence.
His hatband is red,
there is red in her lips and in the handles

of the bureau which contains what few rags
they own. He never
stands still, there is electricity in the air,

a happy éclat. Even at day's zenith,
the patina is so thick,
nothing real can break through.

❖HARROWER

Across town in a bare studio a woman
sprawls on a cot in a scratch of black.
She knows nothing of your ultimates,
the blacks of her railing down, yellowing

her skin, the mattress, the wooden floor,
until all turns honeyward that had been
hardness, and she tilts through midnight
with no maxim to anchor her. You,

happy harrower, haunted in gabardine
by the river where you smell the tannic acid,
smoke and calfskins of the leather factory;
no longer beholden to one behind a pale window

whom you left, if only for the November trees
that turn your head behind split-level homes,
if only that telephone poles not church spires
trawl the sky for you, that molybdenum sky,

where you walk the broken sidewalk, where
you find your abysses. Beneath umber
shingles of stuccoed markets and slate walls
of warehouses stained green in misty air

that breathes *teutonic* in your ear, and lights
the tungsten in your eyes—you feel that love
of everything alive, verily, of the volatile.
Lord of minstrels and minerals, you, the harrower.

And threescore thousand Norsemen couldn't drag
your mongrel spirit from its junkyards and garages
below a staved-in sky and branches swagging
their heavy browns, hard as bones in barnyards,

as they peak into the white. Not yet has love
derailed you from the path of cracked cement
in which you read the book of yourself—
or rather, of what you may become.

◈SLOWLY, SLOWLY, HORSES

Night designs a darkness of horseweed.
Without this fear
in me I would not know where to be.
The field is steeped
in darkness where the horses died.
I would not know
how to be silent. Something cold grooms
what's left of their hides,
the tussocked weeds, and it is not, no,
it is never the wind.
If it were the wind, I would hear it the way
a drowning man
tastes water, the way a horse remembers
grass, the cramp of colic.
Night is nothing but night before red
spiders foam
from its mouth, before horses paw
the dirt at dawn.
Give them room to breathe, I say.

I rode bareback once in a brown lake;
they couldn't see us
from the house, couldn't save us if
we went down.
Mountains loomed around and *no one,*
I promised myself,

no one ever again. My mouth made
the slack shape
water makes when something falls into it.

Night is such a furled feminine thing
around the muscles
of horses, the nettles in their fetlocks,
it is nothing
but the night before and the night after,
only starrier,
uglier. I try to shake them from it, take
their pain away,
they're dirty, I think, *I'll make them clean.*
It goes cold
again as horsetails lash the air; shadows
hemorrhage
in the heart of the field, flooding it, and I flee.
All night long
I see the violent iron frowns of horseshoes.
Someday this pasture
will be pavement. See the barbed wire?
See the weeds?
Once I had a breath I did not breathe.

III.

◇PORTRAITS

1. Bird-Watcher

The sky's cool skin was caftaned in fog
and for days
the fields were rainfragrant.

Near a scrim of leaves, in the theater
of furzeblades,
she touched her collarbone like an actress

pretending to be inside her own skin.
Later, the leaves
went cochineal and the air carried

the smell of burnt sugar and cloves.
Earth gone rusty
with pumpkins and snuffed fires,

did I hear a door close? I honed my thoughts
on death's whetstone
as words fell from her like pieces of a mask.

We waited for hawks but only saw a kettle
of vultures riding
a draft as crows chiselled the silence with cries.

I tried to ignore it, but it was then that I felt
the season engraved
by the scrimshaw blade of the wind.

2. Beauty Queen

Pleasure is death's stalking-horse.
As noted by
the quondam girl-of-the-year who lies

in bed wrapped in a stole of ostrich
feathers, her face
a wasted columbine, a dove's face but

a frozen one from which eyes stare
like drilled blanks.
For whom the taste of wormwood

is delayed, but when it comes, it comes
as an epiphany
of bitterness not even twenty kid-gloved

chaperones nor thoroughbreds can
spare her.
And all her gauze has shrivelled

to a knot that flavors her words metallic
and that cannot,
as she smooths her silk camisole, be spat out—

she needs it now as an eye gives her
the once-over
and the horse moves closer and closer.

3. *Trojan*

If I were a more serious mistress
of the dark legions,
perhaps I'd know you, wounded one,

why all that blood was for nothing,
why your
ultras ring true even so. What gods

were hailed in your ear? How did the sea-
winds take you?
A skull for a skull under the sky's endlessness.

In the rain of gore, a grub might have been
the fulcrum
on which victory shifted. A grub

in a field smelling of bronze—implacable.
Which woman
were you forced to forget as you choked

down a mess of grief at each meal?
Hero as lover
and butcher: what agonies en suite?

Earth was crawling with gods and worms.
We eat
what still flowers from archaic hearts.

❖ET IN ARCADIA EGO

There is no way to escape arcadia.
I am truly gone, over the border.
In dank air, clouds make a thick soup
of the sky. No one will come to the door.

Trashbags pile up on the fire escape
as people inside drink another toast
to themselves. The roads, obscured
by snow, are steep as a man's last breath.

Were there a way out, I'd ignore it.
Sky over mountains the color of ash.
I descry the face of one who calls me
as the water in my cup turns brackish.

The bricks of the house begin to look
more like tiny caskets than cakes of wheat.
Deer stamp a trail in snow like a rope
I could follow home, but it is frayed.

So frayed, I'd never find my way in time.
Lives are lived in this valley. I have miles
of space here but can travel nowhere far.
Our eyes will be closed for thousands of years.

I catch a glimpse. I know we have spoken.
And we will, and mud will take us intently.
Cold for a moment, I can see across:
· it tells me winters and summers.

◇ THE ASTRONOMER

I eat stars, breathe stars, bathe in stars.
I dream incoherent dreams of comets,
asteroids, and lunar Alps. Becoming
myself a satellite, I orbit the shrine

of a holy sun, tracing for all time an egg-
shaped pilgrimage through gelid space.
I see the city as through a telescope:
streetlamps glow, contracted white dwarfs.

The hemisphere unveils for me its sheer
and empty skull of glass as leaves crinkle
in the cold dark outside the planetarium.
At times, Polaris seems to leak skim milk,

the Pleiades are plotting their escape,
and Betelgeuse burns Orion's shoulder.
Priest of distances, I've mastered the art
of leaving hope and human shores behind.

Or has it mastered me? Even the moon
wears her evanescence on her sleeve.
What is it in me always trying to flee
across spaces coldblooded, godless?

It is a mood of blue magnified by solitude.
A solitude magnified by the sight of stars,
the stars I see through the telescope lens,
the stars, nomadic planets, and the moon.

◊ GREEN

In the park, by a shoal of minnows in a sun-
patch of creekwater and fluted bells of virginia
waterleaf, you feel the sun transfix you,

see picnickers revel with gauds and grills.
And in this heat you lance the thick,
pollen-glazed air with thoughts of another

perhaps just now awakening to a difficult air.
The body no longer a topos of projected dreams,
perfectibilities, now a scar of fodder and harrows

and hay, and all the sic transits and slackenings
of late summer, the green hamartia of youth.
What do you say as blackbirds rise from the brush—?

Not far from here the bones of strangers
lie in depleted light where you seek,
among the pendant greens and reddish petals,

redemption in the pith of solitude, to know
the violence of the brightest day
and witness its transfiguration into gray.

◇PROPHET OF WOE

Nimrod of the night, I am
an avian *prophete of wo & of*
        myschaunce. From pole

to pole I range the globe
in noiseless flight nocturnal,
        my plumage shadow-soft.

Dauntless in any weather,
with talons sharp as augers,
        and a beak like a carpenter's awl.

In this workshop of branches,
I am the brain and eyes of the forest.
        Rats, snakes, and dragonflies

betray themselves to my ready
wits. Hissing, ferny, church,
        snowy, woodcock, bare-toed,

october. Formerly known as
Athene noctua, guardian
        of the Acropolis. Augurs read

mischief as my tidings: *screech-*
witch, monster of the night.
        Do not bring me to Athens—

they carved my head on their coins.
My eggs, they said, cure
            intemperance; my heart

        is a talisman of truth. Only darkness
coaxes me from brooding mime
            of tree branch, leaf cluster.

        The sun repels me with its
brazen stare. It is the moon,
            aloof and fruitless, I admire.

◈ THE PRODIGAL

In the illness of surfeit, I've seen through
the legerdemain of doctors, the placebos
they're forever pulling from their pockets.
I long for sleep, that dark pharmacy

with its shelves of empty bottles.
Dawn hauls its ruddy load over the hill.
Cars rasp along, antagonizing trees.
One can't escape the past; I know—I tried.

Hard to believe how soon these cups were drained.
I would fain have eaten husks fit for swine.
This split I've got down the middle prevents
me from knowing myself. At least the tree

I lean against feels solid. When one gets
close enough to anything, all one sees
are lacunae. It's good to see the holes,
but not to fall through them, as I do now.

The willow droops its tenebrous crown at me.
As though it told me so—how odious.
Night, an obsidian satyr, has cantered off
to other lands. All day I lay in pieces.

The pulchritude of angels leaves me cold;
their world will never intersect with mine.
This morning, I lost my way in seeking
the scope of forests where branches stutter

in an arid wind's locust-bearing gusts.
Now a tattered No coils back on itself,
a wastrel shroud scarring the horizon
where clouds pile up like fatted calves on altars.

◆POLITICIAN

Along dark streets splashed silver by the moon
you stumble, dreaming up flags to impale
the rarefied air. Cars slink along the curbs.

Needles of light quiver on the hubcaps
and bumpers; parking meters stand in line
like voters with bludgeoned eyes. Your mind

goes gray as the cobblestones, chainlink fences,
tenement houses of Mechanicsville, Guernsey,
whatever district you're passing through now.

Were the weather to turn malevolent,
it would only strengthen your resolve.
Shadows bunch like leeches sucking the light.

Ideas hum, electric, through your neurons
and mandates galvanize your heart
while back in your office, a lightbulb—

spare, your last one, blinking—scatters
its dry flakes like a small god spreading lies.
You raise incarnadine flags that billow

in northerly winds as you march along
deserted roads white with the milk of stars.
You could comb those roads forever and

no diesel would open its doors for you.
No curbside caresses; only these dreams,
inarticulate, and clouds like tumid udders.

If only you could give blood to such vapors!
But even now you feel the mouth of knowledge
opening to the mouth of uncertainty.

◈ THE LAUGHER

I laugh without a mouth.
My lunar death-mask disturbs
the air around me like
a stone dropped in water.
It is you I watch with inky,
lidless eyes: these oval
hollows through which the dark
that pools around me leaks.
Am I drowning? Or rising
to gasp for air? Inscrutable
marble harlequin—I do
not give myself away—

cipher, schwanengesang,
sycophant of snow and ground
zero. I deny, I deny.
Muteness smothers my mouth.
Dignity of silence! The arch
erotics of a cygnus neck!
And see what's trapped in these
tar-pit eyes, taboo holes
in a sacerdotal mask.
No one belongs to this tribe.
I become whomever looks
at me: a reverse Narcissus.

I, a conduit, a mocking
cavity, an ivory dice—
decipher me, forewarned.
Whatever objects you place
in the smooth bowl of my face—
they all vanish quietly.
For years I strove for the sheen
of lustrous metals; I laved
away the scars and debris
that once had draped necklaces
of cowrie shells, ceramic
beads, and leopard teeth
around my life—ornamental,
but outlandish in their clatter.

◇MISÈRE DES HÔTELS

Amok in the dialectic mess of the streets,
its mad choreography of hands and feet,

how can I look at the sky and not want it?
Its star-tortured skin so far out of whack

with signs of a storm before the storm comes.
Day after day I don my face like a uniform.

Amok in the oceanic gross-out of roaches,
broken meats—the palaces of Machu Picchu

despoiled of lavishness and the black ware
of lesser gods and a silver llama—I, an heir

to this legacy of track-lit chaff and char,
this potsherd world of power-lunch smut.

Love is a speck in these boroughs of glizt
defaced with each night's graffiti. How will I

know who speaks when you turn to me from
the ex nihilos of your mind? When the city

opens its drains, even the dead are displaced,
orphaned and spreading their tarnished coins.

❖ WANHOPE

I flee a house of torpor, of mummies,
the smell of camphor and mothballs.

In the forest, the quilled arms
of the aspen drop incense all around.

Rabbits nose a patch of fallen berries
near a smattering of fewmets beneath ferns.

I seek asylum of hell-dark, to be healed.
In cones of moonlight, bats loop out

with a licorice sheen as my flashlight
glances off trees and rocks, whorls

of gloom unfolding before it. But a beam
can only extend so far before its photons

flake off in the mouth of darkness.
Darkness eats anything—I confess, I fly into it.

Is it the seethe of wasp-wings in the brush,
or the wind's dissonance in fretted leaves?

To the halaloo of a hoot-owl I wallow on
until I become a runnel of the black

rivers that swathe the pulp of trees—
all this opacity receives me.

Dead beasts fester among briars,
primitive murk—the rocks wear their skin—

and as the rowels of my fear wind down,
the clods of earth disclose to me a new grammar.

◈SCARRED

Clouds flake off piece by piece above the rough
ice-collared snow, the slags of light in soil.

The splay of tree-crowns spurring and furling
up into the sky. Black boughs in glacial ache.

Husks of bark, of shivered wood moored on ice;
fringe of it receding from pools of blue,

the pools having taken the sheen of sky
down to their depths. Palest of white ridges

infolding, asphalt bastioned with furrows
along the field of it. Scarred with dead blades,

the world withdraws in white before me.
Frost's multi-angled effacements—nothing

made fast is what I have: the atrophy
of leaf and sap, the waste and feed of it.

◈ NERVE-LIKE

Palest ice-shard blue of sky, of arctic glass.
Crust of snow like meerschaum over the yard.
Branches crosshatch a chiasma of lines
in snow. Can blue so liquid be transmuted,
those sluices of shadow and soft rivers
of light that splash against the candelabrum
of branches? The louvered incrustations
of ice, the lost geometries of snow,
this deep into winter no uniform white,
just the mottled seepages of blue down
in cracks, the sky going gray in nerve-like
patches, fadings into and out of blueness
and the flooding of that in vein-colored
branches, the bark husked by some violence.

◇AIRS OF MIDDLE NIGHT

The sky pokes a black finger
through a wormhole in a leaf

where a nightingale's eye had glinted.
We no longer speak of the sky,

though carnations tilt in a vase:
a clump of shunted hydra-heads,

they reek of astrology.
The nightingale no longer sings

where snakes jerk through convolutions
of dead petals, though a tint

of its plumage flares
across the sky and lingers

like the perfume of a woman
who has rushed from the room.

◇SEAPIECES

I.

A week of black hues—hot cabanas.
I hear at times odd horsehair bows scrape
swarmy notes where sea is both that selfsame
sea and alchemist of conch shells & dead
sailors. *Can I never see and not be seen?*
Not these death-fostering waves of light
nor filigrees—but this rasping, rosined
smell lures me back to reality. O fabliau
(I bow obsoletely) of palm-fronds,
hibiscus leaves, pelicans:...O mother
in a white scarf gesturing by the surf,
into the ultramarine a boy is wading.

II.

Is not my mind a mind to behold
a colossus in a curved pink shell?
To pine & seek repose in muttering waves?
I sit in bad light in a bed of shells.
My sense of life has fear (with manic claws)
torn to shreds...with like confusion & lack
terns ransack sargassum weeds. *Cannot
reach me,* I think, as other things (crabs,
mollusks) rot: all along the sand hotels:
the stench of which binds me there like cuffs.
Darkly daunted mind—from racket and
whisk of spray I try and try to turn away.

III.

Pelicans twist, v-shaped wings akimbo,
into the sea—its coruscating green
expressions on which a speedboat carves
a foamy scar—white-hot, too harsh.
I want back, want away, a sabbath
of shadow and solitude. Not this sun
with copper threads stitching me nerve by
nerve to the cabana, not this Sardanapalus
posed in guava light like a nursemaid
bearing salves. Pelicans, at least, know
what they're after: shadows on the water:
shadows—protean & momentary.

IV.

Apropos of music—i.e., cracked flutes
of gulls and intonations of the sea—
I hear litanies without surcease
of too-much-sun. Or might those waves
be cutlasses brandished by pirates
in the high seas' glitter & subsume?
When those blades clash do they, outlandishly,
mirror a (mutant, at-war, unspeakable)
part of the self? Seasick I seek an anchor
in the blue that heaves me from its blank
horizon: I make of those displacements
what I can: at last, at least, an answer.

ACKNOWLEDGEMENTS

Grateful acknowledgement is made to the editors of the following publications, in which some of these poems originally appeared:

Cimarron Review: "Harrower"
Colorado Review: "Nerve-Like" (as "Palest Ice-Shard Blue"), "Scarred" (as "Clouds Flake Off")
The Gettysburg Review: "A House of Cards", "Portraits", "Folie à Deux"
Gulf Coast: "Birdlight"
Iowa Journal of Cultural Studies: "Gamblers"
The Iowa Review: "Palinode", "The Astronomer", "The Prodigal"
Mid-American Review: "Iowa River, 8/9/99"
Parnassus: "Clouds Swell Out"
Pequod: "Seapieces"
Poet Lore: "Invocation"
Seneca Review: "Alexander the Great" and "Prophet of Woe"
Southwest Review: "Slowly, Slowly, Horses"

I wish to thank the Vermont Studio Center and the James Michener Foundation for their support. Thanks also to the many whose advice and criticism has helped to shape these poems, especially to Marvin Bell, Chase Twichell, and Jorie Graham.

"Invocation" was influenced, in form, by Frank Bidart's poem "The Yoke."

The phrase "slowly, slowly, horses" is taken from Ovid's *The Art of Love*, Book I, Chapter XIII.

The italicized line in "Days of No Luster" was adapted from the first chapter of *Alchemy: The Medieval Alchemists and Their Royal Art* by Johannes Fabricius.

In "Prophet of Woe," the first italicized lines are adapted from Chaucer's "The Legend of Good Women: The Legend of Philomela."

Line 15 of "Concordia Discors" was influenced by a sentence from St. Augustine's *Confessions*. This poem first appeared in a limited-edition chapbook published by Inflorescence Press.